In "Flourless Delights," explore the limitless possibilities of flour-free baking and embark on a delicious journey that challenges conventional norms. This cookbook presents an array of tantalizing recipes that prove you don't need flour to create decadent treats. From moist cakes to shortbreads, each recipe is meticulously crafted to deliver the perfect balance of flavours and textures. With easy-to-follow instructions and a pantry-friendly approach, "Flourless Delights" equips you with the tools to embrace a flour-free lifestyle while satisfying your cravings for baked goods. Unleash your creativity in the kitchen and discover the joy of flourless baking with this captivating collection of recipes.

Copyright

All rights reserved. No part of this cookbook may be reproduced, distributed, or transmitted in any form or by any means, including photocopying, recording, or other electronic or mechanical methods, without the prior written permission of the publisher, except in the case of brief quotations embodied in critical reviews and certain other noncommercial uses permitted by copyright law.

Disclaimer

The recipes provided in this cookbook are for informational purposes only. The author and publisher of this cookbook make no representations or warranties regarding the accuracy, completeness, or reliability of the information contained in these recipes. The recipes are provided "as is" and without any warranties, express or implied.

The reader assumes full responsibility for any actions taken based on the information provided in this cookbook. The author and publisher shall not be held liable for any damages or injuries arising from the use of the recipes or any other information contained in this cookbook.

It is the reader's responsibility to exercise caution and use their own judgment when preparing and consuming the recipes in this cookbook, especially in cases of allergies, dietary restrictions, or specific health conditions. It is recommended to consult a qualified healthcare professional or nutritionist for personalized advice regarding dietary needs and restrictions.

The inclusion of specific products, brands, or websites in this cookbook does not imply endorsement or sponsorship. Any mention of such entities is solely for informational purposes and does not constitute a formal endorsement.

Always follow proper food safety guidelines and hygiene practices when handling and preparing ingredients.

Content

1. Introduction
2. Dedication
3. Alternative ideas for ingredients
4. Conversions
5. Nutritional Requirements
6. Chocolate Cake
7. Strawberry Coconut Cake
8. Almond Flour Cake
9. Carrot Cake with Oat Flour
10. Peanut Butter Banana Cake
11. Lemon and Almond Cake
12. Apple Cinnamon Cake with Oat Flour
13. Orange and Almond Cake
14. Black Bean Chocolate Cake
15. Carrot Cake with Cashew Cream Frosting
16. Banana and Coconut Cake
17. Peanut Butter Chocolate Chip Cake
18. Lemon and Poppyseed Cake
19. Strawberry Shortcake
20. Blueberry Lemon Cake with Almond Flour
21. Chocolate Zucchini cake
22. Carrot Cake with Cream Cheese Frosting
23. Coconut Pineapple Upside Down Cake
24. Pumpkin Spice Cake with Almond Flour
25. Sweet Potato Cake with Coconut Flour
26. Chocolate Avocado Cake
27. Strawberry Coconut Cake
28. Zucchini Cake with Oat Flour
29. Hazelnut Flour Cake with Nutella Frosting
30. Banana Walnut Cake with Oat Flour
31. Vanilla Coconut Cake with Coconut Flour
32. Raspberry Almond Cake
33. Chocolate Chip Banana Cake with Oat Flour

Introduction

Indulge in guilt-free cakes with our flour-free recipe book! Our collection of more than 20 easy and delicious cakes is perfect for gluten-free, paleo, or low-carb diets. Made with wholesome ingredients and no refined sugars, each cake is moist, fluffy, and bursting with unique flavours and textures.

With step-by-step instructions and helpful tips, our recipe book is perfect for novice and experienced bakers alike. From classic chocolate cake to zesty lemon cake and fruity berry cake, our cakes are sure to impress your family and friends. Discover the secret to baking up a storm and treat yourself to the sweet pleasure enjoy the rich flavors and aromas of our flour-free cakes today!"

To the Unforgettable Sheroes,

This book is dedicated to all the incredible women who have been by my side, holding my hand through the ups and downs, the victories and defeats, and even the silly moments that make life worth living. You are the ones who have cheered me on, believed in me when I doubted myself, and reminded me of my strength when I felt weak.

You have been my rock, my confidante, and my source of endless inspiration. Your unwavering support has lifted me up and given me the courage to face any challenge that comes my way. You have shown me the true meaning of friendship, sisterhood, and the power of a kind and loving heart.

Through every trial and tribulation, you have stood tall by my side, reminding me of my worth and helping me find my voice. You have celebrated my triumphs as if they were your own and shared in the joy of my accomplishments. Your belief in me has fueled my dreams and pushed me to reach for the stars.

But it's not just the big moments that matter—it's also the laughter-filled, silly moments we've shared that have etched memories in my heart forever. Whether it's late-night dance parties, inside jokes, or spontaneous adventures, you have brought lightness and joy to my life. You've shown me the importance of cherishing the small moments and finding delight in the everyday.

So, to all the amazing sheroes in my life, this book is a testament to the love, laughter, and unwavering support you have given me. It is a tribute to your resilience, kindness, and beautiful spirits that have touched my life in ways words cannot express.

May these pages inspire you as you have inspired me. May they bring warmth to your soul, a smile to your face, and a reminder of the incredible woman you are. Together, let us continue to uplift and empower one another, I know we can conquer anything that comes our way.

With boundless love and gratitude,

MaGumbo - CS

Alternative Ingredients

Alternative ideas for ingredients

Coconut flour is a unique ingredient because it absorbs a lot of liquid and provides a lot of fibre to baked goods. If you can't use coconut flour, it's best to use a different recipe that doesn't rely on this ingredient.

- However, if you want to experiment with substitutions, you can try using almond flour or another nut flour in its place. Keep in mind that almond flour is not a 1:1 substitution for coconut flour, so you may need to adjust the amount of liquid in the recipe to get the right consistency.

- Other gluten-free flour like rice flour, tapioca flour, or potato starch can also be used, but they may not provide the same texture as coconut flour. So, it's best to experiment with small batches first to see how the recipe turns out with different substitutions.

Alternative ideas for ingredients

There are several nut-free flour alternatives that can be used in baking. Here are some options:

- **Rice flour:** Made from finely ground rice, it's a good option for people with nut allergies. It's commonly used in gluten-free baking.

- **Oat flour:** Made from ground rolled oats, it's a good source of fibre and protein. It can be used as a substitute for wheat flour in many recipes.

- **Tapioca flour:** Made from the root of the cassava plant, it's a starchy flour that can add texture and thickness to recipes. It's often used in gluten-free baking.

- **Potato starch:** Made from the starch extracted from potatoes, it's a good alternative to wheat flour for thickening sauces or soups. It can also be used in baking as a gluten-free flour substitute.

- **Corn flour:** Made from ground corn, it can be used in baking and cooking. It's often used in cornbread, tortillas, and tamales.

It's important to note that some of these flours may not work well in all recipes, and you may need to experiment with different ratios to get the right texture and consistency. Also, some people with nut allergies may also be allergic to other ingredients, so it's important to read labels carefully and consult with a healthcare professional if you have any concerns.

Alternative ideas for ingredients

In these recipes, coconut oil is used as a healthy fat that also adds moisture to the cakes. If you prefer not to use coconut oil, you can replace it with other healthy fats such as olive oil, avocado oil, or melted butter. However, keep in mind that this may slightly alter the taste and texture of the cakes. So, if you're looking for a coconut-free option, you can try using one of these alternatives and adjust the amount according to your preference.

- **Olive oil:** It has a mild flavour that works well in baking and is a healthy option.

- **Avocado oil:** It is a rich oil with a neutral flavour that is perfect for flourless cakes.

- **Grapeseed oil:** It has a neutral flavour and is good for high-temperature baking.

- **Canola oil:** It is a light oil with a neutral flavour that is a popular choice for baking.

- **Sunflower oil:** It is a light oil with a mild flavour that works well in flourless cakes.

- **Walnut oil:** It has a nutty flavour that adds a unique taste to cakes.

It's important to note that different oils may have different smoke points and flavour profiles, so it's important to choose the right oil for the recipe you are following.

Conversions

1 Cup (Liquid Ingredients):
Metric: 1 cup = 250 milliliters (ml)
Imperial: 1 cup = 8 fluid ounces (fl oz) = 237 milliliters (ml)

1/2 Cup:
Metric: 1/2 cup = 125 milliliters (ml)
Imperial: 1/2 cup = 4 fluid ounces (fl oz) = 118 milliliters (ml)

1/4 Cup:
Metric: 1/4 cup = 60 milliliters (ml)
Imperial: 1/4 cup = 2 fluid ounces (fl oz) = 59 milliliters (ml)

3/4 Cup:
Metric: 3/4 cup = 180 milliliters (ml)
Imperial: 3/4 cup = 6 fluid ounces (fl oz) = 177 milliliters (ml)

2/3 Cup:
Metric: 2/3 cup = 160 milliliters (ml)
Imperial: 2/3 cup = 5.3 fluid ounces (fl oz) = 158 milliliters (ml)

1 Cup (Dry Ingredients):
Metric: 1 cup = 240 grams (g)
Imperial: 1 cup = 8.45 ounces (oz) = 227 grams (g)

1/2 Cup:
Metric: 1/2 cup = 120 grams (g)
Imperial: 1/2 cup = 4.23 ounces (oz) = 113 grams (g)

1/4 Cup:
Metric: 1/4 cup = 60 grams (g)
Imperial: 1/4 cup = 2.12 ounces (oz) = 57 grams (g)

3/4 Cup:
Metric: 3/4 cup = 180 grams (g)
Imperial: 3/4 cup = 6.35 ounces (oz) = 170 grams (g)

2/3 Cup:
Metric: 2/3 cup = 160 grams (g)
Imperial: 2/3 cup = 5.64 ounces (oz) = 151 grams (g)

Daily Nutritional Requirements by Gender and Age:

The following are general guidelines for daily nutritional requirements based on gender and age. Keep in mind that individual needs may vary based on activity level, health conditions, and other factors. These values are based on a 2,000 calorie diet and are approximate recommendations.

Please note that these are general recommendations, and it is always best to consult with a healthcare professional or registered dietitian for personalized nutrition advice based on individual needs and health conditions.

MALE

Age 19-30:

- Calories: 2,500-2,800
- Total Fat: 70-95 grams
- Saturated Fat: Less than 22 grams
- Trans Fat: Less than 2 grams
- Cholesterol: Less than 300 milligrams
- Sodium: Less than 2,300 milligrams
- Total Carbohydrate: 300 grams
- Dietary Fiber: 28-34 grams
- Sugars: Less than 50 grams
- Protein: 56-70 grams

Age 31-50:

- Calories: 2,200-2,700
- Total Fat: 70-78 grams
- Saturated Fat: Less than 20 grams
- Trans Fat: Less than 2 grams
- Cholesterol: Less than 300 milligrams
- Sodium: Less than 2,300 milligrams
- Total Carbohydrate: 275 grams
- Dietary Fiber: 28-34 grams
- Sugars: Less than 50 grams
- Protein: 56-70 grams

Age 51 and older:

- Calories: 2,000-2,400
- Total Fat: 65-78 grams
- Saturated Fat: Less than 20 grams
- Trans Fat: Less than 2 grams
- Cholesterol: Less than 300 milligrams
- Sodium: Less than 2,300 milligrams
- Total Carbohydrate: 225-325 grams
- Dietary Fiber: 22-34 grams
- Sugars: Less than 50 grams
- Protein: 56-70 grams

FEMALE

Age 19-30:

- Calories: 2,000-2,200
- Total Fat: 55-77 grams
- Saturated Fat: Less than 20 grams
- Trans Fat: Less than 2 grams
- Cholesterol: Less than 300 milligrams
- Sodium: Less than 2,300 milligrams
- Total Carbohydrate: 260 grams
- Dietary Fiber: 22-28 grams
- Sugars: Less than 50 grams
- Protein: 46-56 grams

Age 31-50:

- Calories: 1,800-2,200
- Total Fat: 55-73 grams
- Saturated Fat: Less than 20 grams
- Trans Fat: Less than 2 grams
- Cholesterol: Less than 300 milligrams
- Sodium: Less than 2,300 milligrams
- Total Carbohydrate: 225 grams
- Dietary Fiber: 22-28 grams
- Sugars: Less than 50 grams
- Protein: 46-56 grams

Age 51 and older:

- Calories: 1,600-2,200
- Total Fat: 55-73 grams
- Saturated Fat: Less than 20 grams
- Trans Fat: Less than 2 grams
- Cholesterol: Less than 300 milligrams
- Sodium: Less than 2,300 milligrams
- Total Carbohydrate: 180-240 grams
- Dietary Fiber: 22-28 grams
- Sugars: Less than 50 grams
- Protein: 46-56 grams

Chocolate Cake

Nutritional Information (per slice):

- Calories: 320
- Fat: 27g
- Carbohydrates: 20g
- Fiber: 3g
- Protein: 5g

Chocolate Cake

Ingredients

1 cup semisweet chocolate chips
1/2 cup unsalted butter
3/4 cup granulated sugar
1/4 teaspoon salt
1 teaspoon vanilla extract
3 large eggs

Method

1. Preheat the oven to 350°F (180°C). Grease an 8-inch (20 cm) cake pan with butter and line it with parchment paper.
2. In a medium saucepan, melt the chocolate chips and butter over low heat, stirring until smooth.
3. Remove the saucepan from the heat and stir in the sugar, salt, and vanilla extract.
4. Beat the eggs in a separate bowl, and then gradually stir them into the chocolate mixture.
5. Pour the batter into the prepared cake pan and bake for 25-30 minutes or until a toothpick inserted in the centre comes out clean.

Allow the cake to cool before serving.

STRAWBERRY COCONUT CAKE

Nutritional Information (per slice):

- Calories: 280
- Total Fat: 21g
- Saturated Fat: 16g
- Cholesterol: 70mg
- Sodium: 110mg
- Total Carbohydrates: 19g
- Dietary Fiber: 5g
- Sugars: 13g
- Protein: 4g

Strawberry Coconut Cake

Ingredients

2 cups unsweetened shredded coconut
1/2 cup coconut flour
1/2 tsp baking powder
1/4 tsp salt
1/2 cup honey
1/2 cup coconut oil, melted
4 large eggs
1 tsp vanilla extract
1 cup fresh strawberries, chopped
Coconut whipped cream, for topping

METHOD

1. Preheat oven to 350°F (180°C).
2. Grease an 8-inch cake pan with coconut oil.
3. In a large bowl, mix together shredded coconut, coconut flour, baking powder and salt
4. In another bowl, whisk together honey, melted coconut oil, eggs, and vanilla extract until well combined.
5. Add wet ingredients to dry ingredients and mix well.
6. Fold in chopped strawberries.
7. Pour batter into the prepared cake pan and bake for 30-35 minutes, or until a toothpick inserted in the centre comes out clean.
8. Let the cake cool in the pan for 10 minutes, then transfer it to a wire rack to cool completely.
9. Serve with coconut whipped cream and additional fresh strawberries, if desired.

Enjoy your delicious Flourless Strawberry Coconut Cake!

Almond Flour Cake

Nutritional Information (per slice):

Calories: 250
Total Fat: 18g
Saturated Fat: 2g
Trans Fat: 0g
Cholesterol: 50mg
Sodium: 150mg
Total Carbohydrate: 18g
Dietary Fiber: 3g
Sugars: 12g
Protein: 6g

Almond Flour Cake

Ingredients

2 cups almond flour
1/2 cup coconut oil
1/2 cup honey
3 large eggs
1 teaspoon baking powder
1 teaspoon vanilla extract

Method

1. Preheat the oven to 350°F (180°C). Grease an 8-inch (20 cm) cake pan with coconut oil.
2. In a large bowl, mix together the almond flour, baking powder, and salt.
3. In a separate bowl, whisk the eggs, honey, and vanilla extract together.
4. Pour the egg mixture into the dry ingredients and stir until well combined.
5. Pour the batter into the prepared cake pan and bake for 25-30 minutes or until a toothpick inserted in the centre comes out clean.

Allow the cake to cool before serving.

Carrot Cake with Oat Flour

Nutritional Information (per slice):
- Carrot Cake
- Calories: 300
- Fat: 25g
- Carbohydrates: 18g
- Fiber: 4g
- Protein: 5g

Carrot Cake with Oat Flour

Ingredients

2 cups oat flour
1 teaspoon baking powder
1 teaspoon baking soda
1 teaspoon cinnamon
1/4 teaspoon nutmeg
1/4 teaspoon salt
2 cups grated carrots
1/2 cup honey
1/2 cup unsweetened apple sauce
3 large eggs
1 teaspoon vanilla extract

Method

1. Preheat the oven to 350°F (180°C). Grease an 8-inch (20 cm) cake pan with coconut oil.
2. In a large bowl, mix together the oat flour, baking powder, baking soda, cinnamon, nutmeg, and salt.
3. In a separate bowl, whisk the honey, applesauce, eggs, and vanilla extract together.
4. Pour the egg mixture into the dry ingredients and stir until well combined.
5. Fold in the grated carrots until evenly distributed.
6. Pour the batter into the prepared cake pan and bake for 25-30 minutes or until a toothpick inserted in the centre comes out clean.

Allow the cake to cool before serving.

Peanut Butter Banana Cake

Nutritional Information (per slice):
Calories: 270
Total Fat: 16g
Saturated Fat: 3g
Trans Fat: 0g
Cholesterol: 85mg
Sodium: 250mg
Total Carbohydrate: 25g
Dietary Fiber: 3g
Sugars: 14g
Protein: 9g

Peanut Butter Banana Cake

Ingredients

3 ripe bananas, mashed
1 cup creamy peanut butter
2 large eggs
1/4 cup honey
1 teaspoon vanilla extract
1/2 teaspoon baking soda
1/2 teaspoon salt
Optional toppings: sliced bananas, chopped peanuts

METHOD

1. Preheat the oven to 350°F (180°C) and grease a 9-inch (23 cm) cake pan.
2. In a large bowl, combine mashed bananas, peanut butter, eggs, honey, vanilla extract, baking soda, and salt.
3. Mix until well combined and smooth.
4. Pour the batter into the prepared cake pan.
5. Bake for 25-30 minutes or until a toothpick inserted in the center of the cake comes out clean.
6. Allow the cake to cool before slicing and serving.
7. Optional: top with sliced bananas and chopped peanuts.

Enjoy your delicious and healthy flourless Peanut Butter Banana Cake!

Lemon and Almond Cake

Nutritional Information (per slice):

Calories: 280
Total Fat: 22g
Saturated Fat: 8g
Trans Fat: 0g
Cholesterol: 75mg
Sodium: 200mg
Total Carbohydrate: 17g
Dietary Fiber: 3g
Sugars: 12g
Protein: 7g

Lemon and Almond Cake

Ingredients

2 cups almond flour
1/2 cup honey
1/2 cup coconut oil
3 large eggs
2 teaspoons baking powder
1/2 teaspoon salt
Zest of 1 lemon
Juice of 1 lemon

Method

1. Preheat the oven to 350°F (180°C). Grease an 8-inch (20 cm) cake pan with coconut oil.
2. In a large bowl, mix together the almond flour, baking powder, and salt.
3. In a separate bowl, whisk the honey, coconut oil, eggs, lemon zest, and lemon juice together.
4. Pour the egg mixture into the dry ingredients and stir until well combined.
5. Pour the batter into the prepared cake pan and bake for 25-30 minutes or until a toothpick inserted in the center comes out clean.

Allow the cake to cool before serving.

Apple Cinnamon Cake with Oat Flour

Nutritional Information (per slice):
Calories: 180
Total Fat: 4g
Saturated Fat: 1g
Trans Fat: 0g
Cholesterol: 55mg
Sodium: 180mg
Total Carbohydrate: 33g
Dietary Fiber: 3g
Sugars: 14g
Protein: 4g

Apple Cinnamon Cake with Oat Flour

Ingredients

2 cups oat flour
2 teaspoons cinnamon
1 teaspoon baking powder
1/2 teaspoon baking soda
1/4 teaspoon salt
2 cups grated apples
1/2 cup honey
1/2 cup unsweetened applesauce
3 large eggs
1 teaspoon vanilla extract

Method

1. Preheat the oven to 350°F (180°C). Grease an 8-inch (20 cm) cake pan with coconut oil.
2. In a large bowl, mix together the oat flour, cinnamon, baking powder, baking soda, and salt.
3. In a separate bowl, whisk the honey, applesauce, eggs, and vanilla extract together.
4. Pour the egg mixture into the dry ingredients and stir until well combined.
5. Fold in the grated apples until evenly distributed.
6. Pour the batter into the prepared cake pan and bake for 25-30 minutes or until a toothpick inserted in the center comes out clean.

Allow the cake to cool before serving.

Orange and Almond Cake

Nutritional Information (per slice):

Calories: 250
Total Fat: 15g
Saturated Fat: 1.5g
Trans Fat: 0g
Cholesterol: 95mg
Sodium: 50mg
Total Carbohydrate: 23g
Dietary Fiber: 4g
Sugars: 17g
Protein: 8g

Orange and Almond Cake

Ingredients

3 oranges
3 cups almond flour
1 cup granulated sugar
1 teaspoon baking powder
6 large eggs

Method

1. Preheat the oven to 350°F (180°C). Grease an 8-inch (20 cm) cake pan with butter and line it with parchment paper.
2. Place the oranges in a large pot and cover with water. Bring to a boil and simmer for 1 hour.
3. Remove the oranges from the pot and allow them to cool. Once cooled, cut them into quarters and remove any seeds.
4. Place the oranges in a food processor and blend until smooth.
5. In a large bowl, mix together the almond flour, sugar, and baking powder.
6. Beat the eggs in a separate bowl, and then gradually stir them into the almond mixture.
7. Fold in the orange puree until evenly distributed.
8. Pour the batter into the prepared cake pan and bake for 1 hour or until a toothpick inserted in the center comes out clean.

Allow the cake to cool before serving.

Black Bean Chocolate Cake

Nutritional Information (per slice):
Calories: 180
Total Fat: 6g
Saturated Fat: 1.5g
Trans Fat: 0g
Cholesterol: 55mg
Sodium: 180mg
Total Carbohydrate: 27g
Dietary Fiber: 5g
Sugars: 13g
Protein: 7g

Black Bean Chocolate Cake

Ingredients

1 can (15 oz) black beans, drained and rinsed
3 eggs
1/2 cup unsweetened cocoa powder
3/4 cup granulated sugar
1/2 tsp baking powder
1/4 tsp salt
1 tsp vanilla extract
1/2 cup semi-sweet chocolate chips

METHOD

1. Preheat oven to 350°F (175°C) and grease an 8-inch cake pan.
2. In a food processor, puree the black beans until smooth.
3. Add eggs, cocoa powder, sugar, baking powder, salt, and vanilla extract to the black bean mixture. Puree until smooth and well combined.
4. Fold in the chocolate chips.
5. Pour the batter into the prepared pan.
6. Bake for 25-30 minutes or until a toothpick inserted in the center comes out clean.
7. Let the cake cool for 10 minutes before removing it from the pan.
8. Slice and serve.

Enjoy your delicious flourless black bean chocolate cake!

Carrot Cake with Cashew Cream Frosting

For the cashew cream frosting (per serving):

Calories: 180
Total Fat: 16g
Saturated Fat: 7g
Trans Fat: 0g
Cholesterol: 0mg
Sodium: 60mg
Total Carbohydrate: 11g
Dietary Fiber: 1g
Sugars: 7g
Protein: 2g

Nutritional Information (per slice):

Calories: 300
Total Fat: 19g
Saturated Fat: 6g
Trans Fat: 0g
Cholesterol: 70mg
Sodium: 320mg
Total Carbohydrate: 27g
Dietary Fiber: 4g
Sugars: 16g
Protein: 8g

Carrot Cake with Cashew Cream Frosting

Ingredients

For the cake:

2 cups almond flour
1 teaspoon baking powder
1 teaspoon baking soda
1 teaspoon cinnamon
1/2 teaspoon ground ginger
1/4 teaspoon nutmeg
1/2 teaspoon salt
3 large eggs
1/2 cup honey
1/4 cup coconut oil
1 teaspoon vanilla extract
2 cups grated carrots

For the cashew cream frosting:

1 cup raw cashews, soaked in water overnight
1/4 cup honey
1/4 cup coconut oil
1/4 cup almond milk
1 teaspoon vanilla extract
Pinch of salt

Method

To make the Cake:

1. Preheat the oven to 350°F (180°C). Grease an 8-inch (20 cm) cake pan with coconut oil.
2. In a large bowl, mix together the almond flour, baking powder, baking soda, cinnamon, ginger, nutmeg, and salt.
3. In a separate bowl, whisk the eggs, honey, coconut oil, and vanilla extract together.
4. Pour the egg mixture into the dry ingredients and stir until well combined.
5. Fold in the grated carrots until evenly distributed.
6. Pour the batter into the prepared cake pan and bake for 25-30 minutes or until a toothpick inserted in the center comes out clean.
7. Allow the cake to cool before frosting.

To make the cashew cream frosting:

1. Drain the soaked cashews and place them in a blender or food processor.
2. Add the honey, coconut oil, almond milk, vanilla extract, and salt.
3. Blend until the mixture is smooth and creamy.

Once the cake has cooled, spread the cashew cream frosting over the top of the cake.

Banana and Coconut Cake

Nutritional Information (per slice):

Calories: 220
Total Fat: 14g
Saturated Fat: 9g
Trans Fat: 0g
Cholesterol: 65mg
Sodium: 250mg
Total Carbohydrate: 20g
Dietary Fiber: 4g
Sugars: 11g
Protein: 5g

Banana and Coconut Cake

Ingredients

3 ripe bananas, mashed
1/2 cup coconut flour
1/2 cup almond flour
3 large eggs
1/4 cup honey
1/4 cup coconut oil
1 teaspoon baking powder
1/2 teaspoon baking soda
1/4 teaspoon salt
1/2 cup shredded coconut

Method

1. Preheat the oven to 350°F (180°C). Grease an 8-inch (20 cm) cake pan with coconut oil.
2. In a large bowl, mix together the coconut flour, almond flour, baking powder, baking soda, and salt.
3. In a separate bowl, whisk the eggs, honey, and coconut oil together.
4. Pour the egg mixture into the dry ingredients and stir until well combined.
5. Fold in the mashed bananas and shredded coconut until evenly distributed.
6. Pour the batter into the prepared cake pan and bake for 25-30 minutes or until a toothpick inserted in the center comes out clean.

Allow the cake to cool before serving.

Peanut Butter Chocolate Chip Cake:

Nutritional Information (per slice):
Calories: 310
Total Fat: 21g
Saturated Fat: 5g
Trans Fat: 0g
Cholesterol: 45mg
Sodium: 230mg
Total Carbohydrate: 26g
Dietary Fiber: 2g
Sugars: 20g
Protein: 8g

Peanut Butter Chocolate Chip Cake:

Ingredients

1 cup creamy peanut butter
1/2 cup honey
2 eggs
1 teaspoon vanilla extract
1/2 teaspoon baking soda
1/2 teaspoon salt
1/2 cup chocolate chips

METHOD

1. Preheat oven to 350°F (180°C) and grease an 8-inch (20 cm) cake pan.
2. In a large bowl, mix together peanut butter, honey, eggs, vanilla extract, baking soda, and salt until well combined.
3. Fold in chocolate chips.
4. Pour batter into prepared cake pan and smooth out the top.
5. Bake for 25-30 minutes or until a toothpick inserted into the center comes out clean.
6. Let cool for 10 minutes before slicing and serving.

Enjoy your delicious flourless Peanut Butter Chocolate Chip Cake!

Lemon and Poppy Seed Cak

Nutritional Information (per slice):

Calories: 260
Total Fat: 18g
Saturated Fat: 6g
Trans Fat: 0g
Cholesterol: 70mg
Sodium: 180mg
Total Carbohydrate: 20g
Dietary Fiber: 3g
Sugars: 13g
Protein: 7g

Lemon and Poppy Seed Cake

Ingredients

2 cups almond flour
1/4 cup coconut flour
1/2 cup honey
1/4 cup coconut oil
3 large eggs
1/4 cup lemon juice
1 tablespoon lemon zest
2 teaspoons poppy seeds
1 teaspoon baking powder
1/4 teaspoon baking soda
1/4 teaspoon salt

Method

1. Preheat the oven to 350°F (180°C). Grease an 8-inch (20 cm) cake pan with coconut oil.
2. In a large bowl, mix together the almond flour, coconut flour, baking powder, baking soda, and salt.
3. In a separate bowl, whisk the eggs, honey, coconut oil, lemon juice, and lemon zest together.
4. Pour the egg mixture into the dry ingredients and stir until well combined.
5. Fold in the poppy seeds until evenly distributed.
6. Pour the batter into the prepared cake pan and bake for 25-30 minutes or until a toothpick inserted in the center comes out clean.

Allow the cake to cool before serving.

Strawberry Shortcake

Nutritional Information (per slice):

Calories: 320
Total Fat: 22g
Saturated Fat: 12g
Trans Fat: 0g
Cholesterol: 70mg
Sodium: 190mg
Total Carbohydrate: 26g
Dietary Fiber: 6g
Sugars: 16g
Protein: 8g

Strawberry Shortcake

Ingredients

1 1/2 cups almond flour
1/2 cup coconut flour
1/2 cup honey
1/4 cup coconut oil
3 large eggs
1 teaspoon baking powder
1/4 teaspoon baking soda
1/4 teaspoon salt
1 cup sliced strawberries
1 cup whipped coconut cream

Method

1. Preheat the oven to 350°F (180°C). Grease an 8-inch (20 cm) cake pan with coconut oil.
2. In a large bowl, mix together the almond flour, coconut flour, baking powder, baking soda, and salt.
3. In a separate bowl, whisk the eggs, honey, and coconut oil together.
4. Pour the egg mixture into the dry ingredients and stir until well combined.
5. Fold in the sliced strawberries until evenly distributed.
6. Pour the batter into the prepared cake pan and bake for 25-30 minutes or until a toothpick inserted in the center comes out clean.

Once the cake is cool, slice it in half horizontally and spread whipped coconut cream over the bottom layer. Place the top layer on top of the whipped coconut cream and spread more whipped coconut cream over the top.

Blueberry Lemon Cake

Nutritional Information (per slice):

Calories: 290
Total Fat: 20g
Saturated Fat: 8g
Trans Fat: 0g
Cholesterol: 70mg
Sodium: 180mg
Total Carbohydrate: 23g
Dietary Fiber: 5g
Sugars: 15g
Protein: 8g

Blueberry Lemon Cake

Ingredients

2 cups almond flour
1/4 cup coconut flour
1/2 cup honey
1/4 cup coconut oil
3 large eggs
1/4 cup lemon juice
1 tablespoon lemon zest
1 cup blueberries
1 teaspoon baking powder
1/4 teaspoon baking soda
1/4 teaspoon salt

Method

1. Preheat the oven to 350°F (180°C). Grease an 8-inch (20 cm) cake pan with coconut oil.
2. In a large bowl, mix together the almond flour, coconut flour, baking powder, baking soda, and salt.
3. In a separate bowl, whisk the eggs, honey, coconut oil, lemon juice, and lemon zest together.
4. Pour the egg mixture into the dry ingredients and stir until well combined.
5. Fold in the blueberries until evenly distributed.
6. Pour the batter into the prepared cake pan and bake for 25-30 minutes or until a toothpick inserted in the center comes out clean.

Allow the cake to cool before serving.

Chocolate Zucchini Cake

Nutritional Information (per slice):

Calories: 260
Total Fat: 18g
Saturated Fat: 9g
Trans Fat: 0g
Cholesterol: 70mg
Sodium: 180mg
Total Carbohydrate: 23g
Dietary Fiber: 6g
Sugars: 14g
Protein: 7g

Chocolate Zucchini Cake

Ingredients

2 cups almond flour
1/2 cup cocoa powder
1/2 cup honey
1/4 cup coconut oil
3 large eggs
1 teaspoon vanilla extract
1/2 teaspoon baking powder
1/2 teaspoon baking soda
1/4 teaspoon salt
1 cup shredded zucchini
1/2 cup dark chocolate chips

Method

1. Preheat the oven to 350°F (180°C). Grease an 8-inch (20 cm) cake pan with coconut oil.
2. In a large bowl, mix together the almond flour, cocoa powder, baking powder, baking soda, and salt.
3. In a separate bowl, whisk the eggs, honey, coconut oil, and vanilla extract together.
4. Pour the egg mixture into the dry ingredients and stir until well combined.
5. Fold in the shredded zucchini and dark chocolate chips until evenly distributed.
6. Pour the batter into the prepared cake pan and bake for 25-30 minutes or until a toothpick inserted in the center comes out clean.

Allow the cake to cool before serving.

Carrot Cake with Cream Cheese Frosting

Nutritional Information (per slice):

Calories: 290
Total Fat: 20g
Saturated Fat: 7g
Trans Fat: 0g
Cholesterol: 60mg
Sodium: 230mg
Total Carbohydrate: 24g
Dietary Fiber: 6g
Sugars: 14g
Protein: 8g

Carrot Cake with Cream Cheese Frosting

Ingredients

For the cake

2 cups almond flour
1/2 cup coconut flour
1/2 cup honey
1/4 cup coconut oil
3 large eggs
1 1/2 cups grated carrots
1/2 cup chopped walnuts
1 teaspoon cinnamon
1/2 teaspoon nutmeg
1 teaspoon baking powder
1/2 teaspoon baking soda
1/4 teaspoon salt

For the frosting

8 ounces of cream cheese, softened
1/4 cup honey
1 teaspoon vanilla extract

Method

1. Preheat the oven to 350°F (180°C). Grease an 8-inch (20 cm) cake pan with coconut oil.
2. In a large bowl, mix together the almond flour, coconut flour, cinnamon, nutmeg, baking powder, baking soda, and salt.
3. In a separate bowl, whisk the eggs, honey, and coconut oil together.
4. Pour the egg mixture into the dry ingredients and stir until well combined.
5. Fold in the grated carrots and chopped walnuts until evenly distributed.
6. Pour the batter into the prepared cake pan and bake for 25-30 minutes or until a toothpick inserted in the center comes out clean.
7. Allow the cake to cool before frosting.

To make the frosting, beat the cream cheese, honey, and vanilla extract together until smooth.
Spread the frosting over the cooled cake and serve.

Coconut Pineapple Upside-Down Cake

Nutritional Information (per slice):

Calories: 340
Total Fat: 22g
Saturated Fat: 16g
Trans Fat: 0g
Cholesterol: 90mg
Sodium: 290mg
Total Carbohydrate: 33g
Dietary Fiber: 5g
Sugars: 25g
Protein: 6g

Coconut Pineapple Upside-Down Cake

Ingredients

1 medium pineapple
1/4 cup butter
1/2 cup brown sugar
1 1/2 cups unsweetened shredded coconut
4 eggs
1/4 cup honey
1/4 cup coconut oil, melted
1/2 cup coconut flour
1/2 tsp baking powder
1/2 tsp salt

Method

1. Preheat oven to 350°F (180°C).
2. Peel and core pineapple, then cut into rings.
3. Melt butter in a cast-iron skillet or oven-safe pan.
4. Add brown sugar to the skillet and stir until dissolved.
5. Arrange pineapple rings in the skillet on top of the brown sugar mixture.
6. Sprinkle shredded coconut evenly over the pineapple rings.
7. In a separate bowl, whisk together eggs, honey, and melted coconut oil.
8. Add coconut flour, baking powder, and salt to the egg mixture and whisk until smooth.
9. Pour cake batter over the pineapple and coconut in the skillet, spreading evenly.
10. Bake for 30-35 minutes, or until cake is golden brown and a toothpick inserted in the center comes out clean.
11. Let cake cool in skillet for 5 minutes before flipping it onto a serving plate.

Serve warm or at room temperature.
Serve with a dollop of whipped cream and fresh berries on top. Enjoy!

Pumpkin Spice Cake

Nutritional Information (per slice):
Calories: 290
Total Fat: 18g
Saturated Fat: 9g
Trans Fat: 0g
Cholesterol: 65mg
Sodium: 190mg
Total Carbohydrate: 27g
Dietary Fiber: 6g
Sugars: 15g
Protein: 7g

Pumpkin Spice Cake

Ingredients

2 cups almond flour
1/2 cup coconut flour
1/2 cup honey
1/4 cup coconut oil
3 large eggs
1 cup canned pumpkin puree
1 teaspoon vanilla extract
1 teaspoon ground cinnamon
1/2 teaspoon ground ginger
1/4 teaspoon ground nutmeg
1/2 teaspoon baking powder
1/2 teaspoon baking soda
1/4 teaspoon salt

Method

1. Preheat the oven to 350°F (180°C). Grease an 8-inch (20 cm) cake pan with coconut oil.
2. In a large bowl, mix together the almond flour, coconut flour, cinnamon, ginger, nutmeg, baking powder, baking soda, and salt.
3. In a separate bowl, whisk the eggs, honey, coconut oil, pumpkin puree, and vanilla extract together.
4. Pour the egg mixture into the dry ingredients and stir until well combined.
5. Pour the batter into the prepared cake pan and bake for 25-30 minutes or until a toothpick inserted in the center comes out clean.

Allow the cake to cool before serving.

sweet potato cake with coconut flour

Nutritional Information (per slice):

Calories: 230
Total Fat: 15g
Saturated Fat: 12g
Cholesterol: 62mg
Sodium: 140mg
Total Carbohydrate: 20g
Dietary Fiber: 4g
Sugars: 13g
Protein: 4g

Sweet potato cake with coconut flour

Ingredients

1 large sweet potato, cooked and mashed
1/2 cup coconut flour
1/2 cup coconut oil, melted
1/2 cup honey or maple syrup
4 eggs
1 tsp vanilla extract
1 tsp baking powder
1/2 tsp salt

Method

1. Preheat the oven to 350°F (180°C). Grease a 9-inch cake pan with coconut oil.
2. In a large mixing bowl, whisk together the sweet potato, coconut flour, coconut oil, honey or maple syrup, eggs, and vanilla extract until smooth.
3. Add the baking powder and salt and whisk until fully incorporated.
4. Pour the batter into the greased cake pan and smooth out the top with a spatula.
5. Bake for 30-35 minutes or until a toothpick inserted into the center of the cake comes out clean.
6. Let the cake cool in the pan for 10 minutes before removing it and letting it cool completely on a wire rack.
7. Serve the cake with a dollop of whipped coconut cream and enjoy!

Enjoy your delicious Cake!

Chocolate Avocado Cake

Nutritional Information (per slice):

Calories: 330
Total Fat: 23g
Saturated Fat: 8g
Trans Fat: 0g
Cholesterol: 80mg
Sodium: 170mg
Total Carbohydrate: 31g
Dietary Fiber: 6g
Sugars: 20g
Protein: 7g

Chocolate Avocado Cake

Ingredients

2 ripe avocados
1 cup semisweet chocolate chips
1/2 cup unsweetened cocoa powder
1/2 cup honey
3 large eggs
1 teaspoon vanilla extract
1/2 teaspoon baking soda
1/4 teaspoon salt

METHOD

1. Preheat the oven to 350°F (175°C) and grease a 9-inch (23cm) cake pan.
2. Melt the chocolate chips over low heat in a small saucepan, stirring occasionally.
3. In a food processor or blender, blend the avocado until smooth.
4. Add the melted chocolate, cocoa powder, honey, eggs, vanilla extract, baking soda, and salt to the avocado puree, and blend until well combined.
5. Pour the batter into the greased cake pan and smooth the top with a spatula.
6. Bake for 25-30 minutes, or until a toothpick inserted in the center comes out clean.
7. Let the cake cool in the pan for 10 minutes, then transfer it to a wire rack to cool completely.
8. Slice and serve with your favourite toppings, such as whipped cream, berries, or chocolate chips.

Enjoy your delicious Flourless Chocolate Avocado Cake!

STRAWBERRY COCONUT CAKE

Nutritional Information (per slice):
Calories: 280
Total Fat: 21g
Saturated Fat: 16g
Cholesterol: 70mg
Sodium: 110mg
Total Carbohydrates: 19g
Dietary Fiber: 5g
Sugars: 13g
Protein: 4g

STRAWBERRY COCONUT CAKE

Ingredients

2 cups unsweetened shredded coconut
1/2 cup coconut flour
1/2 tsp baking powder
1/4 tsp salt
1/2 cup honey
1/2 cup coconut oil, melted
4 large eggs
1 tsp vanilla extract
1 cup fresh strawberries, chopped
Coconut whipped cream, for topping

METHOD

1. Preheat oven to 350°F (180°C).
2. Grease an 8-inch cake pan with coconut oil.
3. In a large bowl, mix together shredded coconut, coconut flour, baking powder, and salt.
4. In another bowl, whisk together honey, melted coconut oil, eggs, and vanilla extract until well combined.
5. Add wet ingredients to dry ingredients and mix well.
6. Fold in chopped strawberries.
7. Pour batter into prepared cake pan and bake for 30-35 minutes, or until a toothpick inserted in the centre comes out clean.
8. Let the cake cool in the pan for 10 minutes, then transfer it to a wire rack to cool completely.
9. Serve with coconut whipped cream and additional fresh strawberries, if desired.

Enjoy your delicious Flourless Strawberry Coconut Cake!

Zucchini Cake with Oat Flour

Nutritional Information (per slice):

Calories: 215
Total Fat: 9g
Saturated Fat: 5g
Trans Fat: 0g
Cholesterol: 70mg
Sodium: 270mg
Total Carbohydrate: 29g
Dietary Fiber: 3g
Sugars: 14g
Protein: 4g

Zucchini Cake with Oat Flour

Ingredients

2 cups grated zucchini
3 eggs
1/2 cup honey
1/3 cup coconut oil, melted
1 teaspoon vanilla extract
1 1/2 cups oat flour
1 teaspoon baking soda
1 teaspoon ground cinnamon
1/2 teaspoon salt
Optional: chopped nuts, dried fruit, or chocolate chips for topping

METHOD

1. Preheat the oven to 350°F and grease a 9-inch cake pan with coconut oil.
2. In a large mixing bowl, whisk together the eggs, honey melted coconut oil, and vanilla extract until well combined.
3. Add the grated zucchini and mix well.
4. In a separate bowl, combine the oat flour, baking soda, cinnamon, and salt.
5. Add the dry ingredients to the wet ingredients and mix until just combined.
6. Pour the batter into the prepared cake pan and smooth out the top.
7. If desired, sprinkle chopped nuts, dried fruit, or chocolate chips on top of the batter.
8. Bake for 35-40 minutes, or until a toothpick inserted into the centre of the cake comes out clean.
9. Allow the cake to cool for 10-15 minutes before slicing and serving.

Enjoy your delicious and healthy Flourless Zucchini Cake with Oat Flour!

Hazelnut Flour Cake with Nutella Frosting

Nutritional Information (per slice):
Calories: 345
Total Fat: 24g
Saturated Fat: 6g
Trans Fat: 0g
Cholesterol: 73mg
Sodium: 252mg
Total Carbohydrate: 29g
Dietary Fiber: 4g
Sugars: 19g
Protein: 8g

Hazelnut Flour Cake with Nutella Frosting

Ingredients

2 cups hazelnut flour
1/2 cup granulated sugar
1/2 cup unsweetened cocoa powder
1 tsp baking soda
1/2 tsp baking powder
1/2 tsp salt
1/2 cup vegetable oil
4 eggs
1 tsp vanilla extract
1/2 cup Nutella
2 tbsp heavy cream

METHOD

1. Preheat oven to 350°F (175°C). Grease an 8-inch cake pan and line with parchment paper.
2. In a large mixing bowl, combine hazelnut flour, granulated sugar, cocoa powder, baking soda, baking powder, and salt. Mix until well combined.
3. In a separate mixing bowl, whisk together vegetable oil, eggs, and vanilla extract until smooth.
4. Add wet ingredients to the dry ingredients and mix until well combined.
5. Pour batter into prepared cake pan and smooth out the surface with a spatula.
6. Bake for 25-30 minutes or until a toothpick inserted into the center comes out clean.
7. Allow the cake to cool in the pan for 10 minutes before transferring it to a wire rack to cool completely.
8. In a small mixing bowl, whisk together Nutella and heavy cream until smooth. Spread the frosting evenly over the cooled cake.

Serve and enjoy!

Banana Walnut Cake with Oat Flour

Nutritional Information (per slice):

Calories: 230
Total Fat: 9g
Saturated Fat: 1g
Trans Fat: 0g
Cholesterol: 62mg
Sodium: 332mg
Total Carbohydrate: 34g
Dietary Fiber: 4g
Sugars: 11g
Protein: 7g

Banana Walnut Cake with Oat Flour

Ingredients

3 ripe bananas, mashed
3 eggs
1/4 cup honey
1 tsp vanilla extract
2 cups oat flour
1 tsp baking soda
1/2 tsp cinnamon
1/2 tsp salt
1/2 cup chopped walnuts

METHOD

1. Preheat the oven to 350°F (175°C) and grease a 9-inch cake pan.
2. In a mixing bowl, combine the mashed bananas, eggs, honey, and vanilla extract.
3. In a separate bowl, whisk together the oat flour, baking soda, cinnamon, and salt.
4. Slowly stir the dry ingredients into the wet mixture until well combined.
5. Fold in the chopped walnuts.
6. Pour the batter into the prepared cake pan and bake for 25-30 minutes or until a toothpick comes out clean.
7. Allow the cake to cool for a few minutes before slicing and serving.

Enjoy your delicious Flourless Banana Walnut Cake with Oat Flour!

Vanilla Coconut Cake with Coconut Flour

Nutrition Information (per slice):
Calories: 310
Total Fat: 19g
Saturated Fat: 14g
Cholesterol: 82mg
Sodium: 133mg
Total Carbohydrates: 30g
Dietary Fiber: 7g
Total Sugars: 19g
Protein: 6g

Vanilla Coconut Cake with Coconut Flour

Ingredients

1 cup coconut flour
1/2 cup unsweetened shredded coconut
1/2 cup honey
1/2 cup coconut oil, melted
1/2 cup unsweetened almond milk
1 tsp vanilla extract
1/2 tsp baking powder
1/4 tsp sea salt
4 large eggs

METHOD

1. Preheat the oven to 350°F. Grease an 8-inch cake pan and line the bottom with parchment paper.
2. In a large bowl, combine the coconut flour, shredded coconut, baking powder, and sea salt.
3. In a separate bowl, whisk together the eggs, honey, coconut oil, almond milk, and vanilla extract.
4. Pour the wet ingredients into the dry ingredients and mix until well combined.
5. Pour the batter into the prepared cake pan and smooth the top with a spatula.
6. Bake for 25-30 minutes or until a toothpick inserted into the center comes out clean.
7. Allow the cake to cool in the pan for 10 minutes before transferring it to a wire rack to cool completely.
8. Optional: top with whipped coconut cream and fresh fruit.

Once the cake has cooled, serve and enjoy!

Raspberry Almond Cake

Nutritional Information (per slice):
Calories: 266
Total Fat: 21g
Saturated Fat: 6g
Trans Fat: 0g
Cholesterol: 62mg
Sodium: 179mg
Total Carbohydrate: 13g
Dietary Fiber: 5g
Sugars: 5g
Protein: 9g

Raspberry Almond Cake

Ingredients

2 cups almond flour
1/2 cup coconut sugar
1 tsp baking powder
1/4 tsp salt
3 eggs
1/4 cup unsweetened almond milk
1/4 cup melted coconut oil
1 tsp vanilla extract
1 cup fresh raspberries

METHOD

1. Preheat oven to 350°F (180°C). Grease an 8-inch round cake pan with coconut oil or line it with parchment paper.
2. In a large mixing bowl, whisk together almond flour, coconut sugar, baking powder, and salt until well combined.
3. In a separate bowl, beat eggs until light and frothy. Add almond milk, melted coconut oil, and vanilla extract and mix until well combined.
4. Pour wet ingredients into the dry ingredients and mix until fully combined.
5. Gently fold in fresh raspberries.
6. Pour batter into the prepared cake pan and bake for 35-40 minutes, or until a toothpick inserted into the centre of the cake comes out clean.
7. Allow the cake to cool in a pan for 10 minutes before transferring it to a wire rack to cool completely.
8. Serve with fresh raspberries and whipped cream, if desired.

Enjoy!

Chocolate Chip Banana Cake with Oat Flour

Nutritional Information (per slice):

Calories: 217
Total Fat: 9g
Saturated Fat: 5g
Trans Fat: 0g
Cholesterol: 32mg
Sodium: 235mg
Total Carbohydrate: 32g
Dietary Fiber: 4g
Sugars: 12g
Protein: 5g

Chocolate Chip Banana Cake with Oat Flour

Ingredients

3 ripe bananas
2 eggs
1/4 cup honey
1/4 cup coconut oil, melted
1 tsp vanilla extract
1 tsp baking soda
1/2 tsp cinnamon
1/4 tsp salt
2 cups oat flour
1/2 cup chocolate chips

Method

1. Preheat the oven to 350°F (175°C) and grease a 9-inch cake pan with cooking spray.
2. In a large mixing bowl, mash the bananas with a fork until smooth.
3. Add the eggs, honey, melted coconut oil, and vanilla extract to the bowl and whisk everything together.
4. Add the baking soda, cinnamon, salt, and oat flour to the bowl and mix until just combined.
5. Fold in the chocolate chips.
6. Pour the batter into the prepared cake pan and smooth out the top with a spatula.
7. Bake for 25-30 minutes or until a toothpick inserted in the center comes out clean.
8. Remove from the oven and let cool for at least 10 minutes before slicing and serving.

Enjoy your delicious flourless chocolate chip banana cake!

www.ingramcontent.com/pod-product-compliance
Lightning Source LLC
Chambersburg PA
CBHW042036100526
44587CB00030B/4446